WHAT
APOCALYPSE?

❦

MARC MCKEE

WHAT
APOCALYPSE?

MARC MCKEE

NEW MICHIGAN PRESS
TUCSON, ARIZONA

NEW MICHIGAN PRESS
DEPT OF ENGLISH, P. O. BOX 210067
UNIVERSITY OF ARIZONA
TUCSON, AZ 85721-0067

<http://newmichiganpress.com/nmp>

Orders and queries to nmp@thediagram.com.

Copyright © 2008 by Marc McKee.
All rights reserved.

ISBN 978-1-934832-17-2. FIRST PRINTING.

Printed in the United States of America.

Design by Ander Monson.

Cover photo © Dominic Arizona Bonuccelli (www.azfoto.com). Used by permission.

CONTENTS

& I Don't Sleep, I Don't Sleep, I Don't Sleep
   Till It's Light   1
At the Edge of a Deep, Dark Wood, Re-Purposed
   Dolphin Speaks   2
This Was During My Animal Rescue Phase   5
Attack Attack   6
We Are All Going to Die, and I Love You   8

*

This Pantsuit Cannot Contain Us   13
Now Then   15
You Think You Will Never Ask to Be Set
   On Fire Again   17
Jason Bredle   19
Jalopy Bellicose   22
I Love You, and We are All Going to Die   25

*

All Souls Procession   29
Bad Move, Simon   31
Child Recruit   33
This Resurrection Costs $4.95   34
O Passenger Manifest   36
Electric Company   39

Acknowledgments   43
Notes   45

for Camellia

*Don't know if I should feel upset or nervous—
will there be a wedding or a funeral service?
We're gathered here today,
we're gathered here today.*

—Panic Strikes a Chord

& I DON'T SLEEP, I DON'T SLEEP, I DON'T SLEEP TILL IT'S LIGHT

A beginning is always a middle pushing through the shape-shaped space
    bored never but with the pause because
surely we are pursued, pursed, the cloaks we've left behind
    cut for blindfolds, the dogs in the distance scorned and starved,

their teeth nervous with the faint taste of our fled heels.
    Bored with being scared, bored with not dying,
the fetching dusk, the becoming sleep. O we are ravenous
    to get ahead of ourselves. O a story this is not

and a story it must be. If I had my way it would be
    a sweet, deep breath drawn slowly in generous peace.
Then a quick exhalation of fire. Hello, space. An appearance of rest only
    while accumulating like a desperate, besotted turbine

that, suddenly set upon, rears high and livid and righteous
    and turns a beauty on them so terrible
those relentless constabularies bearing down on us are babies again,
    reaching out, wanting us to touch their new hands.

AT THE EDGE OF A DEEP, DARK WOOD, RE-PURPOSED DOLPHIN SPEAKS

The they it almost always is
    want to catapult obsolete delivery trucks, elastic plastics,
any extra modern &c into the atmosphere's faults,

the they whose blueprints and schematics whirligig
    so beautifully and fatally
through the softer parts becoming lately late.

            Lately I am desiring my god-effect
but I fear I have had already my god-effect,

a squeak, click, brush of air so someone has the sense of being kissed
    or whispered intensely to just before they woke.
Just as a toe makes a delicious curve

in the saturated sand before the wilderness of the sea,
    so we move in the air of this world
which will cover the dent we made when we leave.

           O, our fortress is on five kinds of fire
but until such expirations as we make

should we not move forward at a keening kneel
    of course already? yes quite thank you here
take my hand. *Fin.* Should we not advance

much celebrant in the throes of nothing
    as in the fantasias of love, budging, stuttering,
gainsaying the fearful knives sketching into the vitalia?

Sure. Convince me. I say the knives are fearful
which is why they are sharp.

Today men who were once
    boys mottling backyards with firecrackers, boys
with equations starring their eyeglasses,

who calculated the vectors of forces diverse
    even being pushed down stairs
are saying *Save the world!* via

            the shooting of stuff into the stratosphere.
    Half a world and 17 degrees of hunger away

a detective soldiery rifles the graveyard
    of a despot's toy box and discovers
a yet-to-be-assembled supergun. At this stage

it is unweird for a dolphin to shimmy loose
    from the approved blossoms
bedecking the mini-mall

            at the edge of a deep, dark wood.
    Now we are certain

we have made too much mention of light,
    now we know we will never be able
to have mentioned it enough.

A poison glides severely
    from each motion we make.
Nothing has ever been this good.

        How else paint the world
but with devouring fire, how else live

              but running with rickshaws full of ice?
    and as one swift and elegant,
                    moving

under the impossible, darling weight of an ocean.

THIS WAS DURING MY ANIMAL RESCUE PHASE

for SB

To be is to be made of glass
that thins over the part that most wants a shield
and so we wade through even a low boil
in search of potential gentles
it's easy to love. Like feral cats.
Minus a vocabulary
anything is easier to love.
A car door is a buckle, a car door is a leap.
One fantasy is rabies.
Another is rushing toward
the burning shoulder of a bridge
to save something that only wants out
of what it can't understand
while the other vehicles hurtle past
like catapulted junkyards filled with orchestras
practicing their minor chords.
Inside you is a thawing tornado maybe
and a raw fist knocking
while you wear your nerves outside your shirt.
You put one foot in front of one foot
in front of one foot in front of one foot
and they are screaming at you now,
there is the peripheral stun of sirens
but you are here,
it is your animal rescue phase
and you reach out to take the wild, terrified thing
into your somehow certain hands.

ATTACK ATTACK

The imperfect products of the nation-state
lose their pitching arms, are torn, kicked loose
in fields of tan roil, the compasses dizzy

amid dreams and despairs
of exostellar clockwork. They have faces
and fall ungently. There. Bereft

of cinema. Salts bring them round
briefly: notions and bodies, magnets
for perforations: just think

of each alien real splitting the skin
into a terrible gasp, think how long it takes
surviving fragments to leach through

the bottom of a coffin, the close room
we wear to the twilight of not being
anymore present—One presumes

until weary and afraid. Sees
a wine bottle slip from stunned fingers.
Sees the sudden blitz of monsoon

coming down in the middle of sheer daylight,
volley after volley of wine bottles
shattering on the streets, on the cars,

beside the baby strollers, please, slicking
the marquees. Carpet. Shards. Prayer.
At the stoplight, between an open window

and the Wig-O-Rama on the corner
shakes a pick-up whose bed
is packed with outmoded wheelchairs

like collapsed accordions. Every available surface
grows an eye. And then it is as if
something red begins to speak.

WE ARE ALL GOING TO DIE AND I LOVE YOU

The world is ending again
    only this time we are sure
which seems to make this time different
    but is actually like every other time

exactly—But! such fantastic plumage of viscera! such spirits
    hot-glued to properties! such a muchness
of dismantled wheels! Really? Our fingertips
    flicker, signing the flickering sky

DESPERATION. How much energy we waste on desperation
    even as we eat of the risotto called into temporary being.
The lovely slinks to the kitchen radio. I am in the past,
    she is pushing a wooden spoon

into an evolving taste that starts moving into us
    light years before. Nothing is still.
To take pleasure in this body and rejoice in the distinctions
    pain provides even as we flee from it

is an experience we kite a host of names for,
    gods of the touch, of the thought, the tongue
a bridge, an accident, reaching but now dinner is done,
    even the evidence has been washed away

and where did it go and we, where goest we?
    We nose into the plastic, becoming histories
in a suit of thorns turned inward like softened fangs.
    Nothing is ever enough. And.

The end is in us—Saturday noon is a year, a year
    is Saturday noon, and the wind shepherds here
the impact of what escapes language, slowly,
    the unstill splinters of a billion billion voices

    and you turn
           and you kiss her
                  right on the mouth—

THIS PANTSUIT CANNOT CONTAIN US

I love how your all-terrain vehicle bursts from the closet
carrying a pipe and admiring itself
in the broken mirror,
I love how it becomes a hummingbird
on the side of a steep hill
refusing to be obliterated by the sun.
I love a thundercloud in a tangerine, the wing of a tree limb
so that you think the trees will be soon aloft
in the unexpected storm,
how your vehicle all-terrain slinks and gnashes,
how the scroll of its wake
seems a superfluous story so discontingent
we throw ourselves into rivers
and at the opening of the cave I love standing
as first a few looping scouts and then a gush of bats
reverse-whirlpool into the sky, the sun bleeding as usual,
invisible cork popped from disfigured champagne bottle,
hundreds of thousands of wobbly, pregnant huntresses
and sudden scatters and breaks
in the swarm/flock/murder/mob/colony's tight formation
like the glue soup of homemade bombs parting
only the screws and nails are quiet and gentle in the air
as drifting sheets of paper.
I love how your all-terrain vehicle's mirrors are ears
and scrape the road when the road is a road
and trembling behind you
more than the ear can hold,
that it can still at this late stage be astonished.
There are those who refuse to believe in the capacity of the body

to withstand, to dole out, to make of soothing a Real
that leaches into other feeling things in existence
but I am not one of them. Exhibit
alphabet: Your all-terrain vehicle. It gets fucked
into giddy moments of oblivion
and I love that. I love the breathing deeply,
the circling back to yourself, the slow dents of cool
in a body after it has been an engine of fire
and how in love, vehicle, in awe, even the air
is a consoling gesture.

NOW THEN

The wound in the first precedent's head
never closes. It floods the multiscape

with impulses that build cities and raze cities,
floods like ceaseless scarves

beyond a novice illusionist's control,
surges through arboretums

like glass blizzards, sups off spine and limb
with an industry for a mouth. We try

standing in ocean, in wave, in wake,
walking into what bends our wings back.

The landings we make are elaborate.
A startling repertoire is required,

a lantern for a heart, a muscular cogito
feeding on the release in stoplights

and sexual rendezvous, their invitations
and stipends. It is all we cannot do

to dance into the mantle
of any savior. Take the neck of a plant

shouldering aside slow-collapsing concrete
and say, griefless and to my face:

We will rescue each moment that enters us.

Fields and city blocks vivify
and fly like glad batteries of cinema

    from our lips: we see them

and then they appear.

YOU THINK YOU WILL NEVER ASK TO BE SET ON FIRE AGAIN

for JW

Curiously, I love it when someone dreams
I have been eaten by a shark.
I love it when someone wakes up sad
that I am a disassemblage
obscured by a cloud of silky red
spooling into water,
failing to make a final obscure joke perhaps—
but especially when anyone wakes
and it turns out I have not been eaten by a shark
do I love it: Think of how many people win!
At least two! and the day
with its sharklessness and unrolling picnic blanket
of bright likelihoods and unlikelihoods
rushes toward horizons that appear toothy
but aren't. It's funny what some days is enough
to make us feel like a pet arrowhead
which I mean in the best way possible
and then how swiftly there seems a sharkishness
beneath the steps we try to manage like Astaire-Rogers
over the contemporary temporary rope bridges.
These endless and big mouths circle
so matter-of-factly, everything seems so hungry
even after feeding, so eager to dress like a palace,
to hoof the thoroughfare
sweating expensive evidence.
Another friend says
scratch consumption and you'll find rage

and of course she's right.
I say scratch rage and you'll find a sadness.
Maybe it is a marriage of our wonder and terror.
You think you won't dive any more
into the deep, cold buffet,
thinking, *I can't believe I get to live this life,*
thinking, *I hate when it pretends to be something else*
but we are called
into the mouth of the night
and we go.

JASON BREDLE

The poem I am writing right now
is called Jason Bredle and the first thing
to happen is the sudden appearance of
the bee whose last gesture is to dive
into meganutricious antioxidant juice
the color of a dozen fruit slashed and squeezed
which reminds me like everything else
of the blood constant. Blood that won't stay
in the lines, blood that marks the doorway
and the lantern, blood in the supermarkets
and in the treads of deflating tires
and the painful pain. Sometimes the painful pain
is in the pieces of the broken bottle
multiplying a reflection one often feels
is unbearable in the singular, sometimes
it is in the bandaged hand in the parking lot
of a huge store chain that radiates hurt
or the eye that won't work and fails
to be diagnosed accurately by every specialist.
Other times the painful pain is painted
on the windows of the vehicle the subject
must own and force to move like blood
through the city's lopsided grid,
which returns us to a need for well-helping
juice so strong we are ready to dive
from the flowers we know into the palace
of a scent we suspect. Tempting others
snake through the city in search of refining
dramas that make them glisten, like the el

crossing paths with Krylon blood-wielding
decorators who make presentable the city.
In any attempt to represent the subject
we move inexorably from the subject.
My subject is Jason Bredle.
He never confuses a horse with a unicorn
and his grammar is the grammar
of the carcass, perfect and jagged
as the crinkles at the coastal borders
which produce such cries for absent mercy
the human appears altogether not. The sea
licks the beach like blood licking the feet.
Sometimes a salary increase helps
but mostly nothing helps.
See that television? Full of painful blood
which makes us very careful around it
lest it be made to open and color the rest
of our lives, to follow us down the stairs
and into the street as if the pain and blood
were on a leash, attached to us by some method
we can't fathom as we wander through the valley
of the carcass. Disease lurks in one petal
and it is the petal that we discover half in
our ice cream sandwich, half in our mouth.
Sometimes disease, sometimes just laughter
we're not sure is coming from our own mouths
which sometimes feel lived in by coppery slither.
There is meditation which doesn't always
make the petal of disease lift from the dark cavern

we throw admirably draping coats and scarves over
in order to get from one part of the city
to the other. But sometimes. And the food
that seems to wait on pedestals of air
as we traverse the network: watch it pass
through us like the painful pain and the blood
and those moments of pleasure and ease
which seem to forgive us, just before the wheel
sprouts the exacting thorns it needs to turn aside
the shield of the pavement. See how vulnerable
the earth is. See how glad we are that the subject
has been able to withstand casual calamity this long
and demented lightning in the circulatory system.
For the subject to hear you he must stand
in a precise corner in a small apartment
but you can detect his presence all the time.
His blades turn stars to dust and demand
from the dust a relapse into bright condition.
Popsicles, ceiling fans, umbrella
parachutes, your aunt and her maladies,
reality television and train stations where
you can't decide on arriving continuously
or departing finally—all are as subject to the painful
pain of the subject as a weeping mother.
A swallow can be a bird and flap its wings
against the hurting, or it can cause
what you waited for to disappear, whether into
the corrosive musculature of the sea
or some other surprising and terrible mouth.

JALOPY BELLICOSE

The teenager's prosthetic limbs get stolen.
Again.
And though time is irresistible and everywhere
with an invisible arsenal
it is even-getting time, somehow.
Where is our string quartet of anti-thieves and anti-cutpurses
to play us into soft battle?
Alarming incisors spin right out of the clouds now
with powers of inversion
such that swimming pools cap sno-cone stands
which would otherwise like the stalks of corn sprout
in the land of our fathers and their dreams,
where they were tattooed and hectored from the town square
into basements, castles inverted and sunk
until the dungeon is finally beloved.
One summer I go in with my hands and rip up the carpet
and the cushion under the carpet
and it's like trying to rip wet sponge
super-glued to a sweaty boulder,
all the while beneath jumbled boxes of trophies
atop small refrigerators, beneath team pictures
of second place finishes, beneath dartboards and deer heads.
The garbage bags we fill are heavy and wet
so it's easy to imagine
we are carrying bodies out to the truck
which reads *Gert's Carpet Cleaners*.
The prosthetic limbs of the teenager again
are stolen. Why is there so much
we must avenge?

Must we set fire to the Camaros
in such a way as to spell out Beautytruth
Truthbeauty? Look at us limping back from the field of play.
We are as effective versus time's challenge scenarios
as a shopping cart with a bad wheel.
I may have said that before. Again. Static creases sky
But can you satisfy your love life co-defendant
with mightiness stamina?! and/or eloquence?
Does your man-tabulation shortfall
less than cunning? Then!
Has myself the catatonic disinhibitor for you? In juice form!
Ahem. The teenager's prosthetic limbs—and I hate to say this, folks,
it's like being the dog that ate grandma's soap sculpture of Roy Rogers—but
the limbs, prosthetic, belonging to the teenager…well,
they've been stolen. Again.
I remember the garbage bags of my youth
as I remember all things of my youth
when the horse of time loses its blindfold and says so.
Time is a Camaro,
stalks of corn are beaten into the ground
like the belated prosthetic limbs of the much-hated teenager.
We are all as teenagers to time,
which is a Camaro with a horse painted on it,
a horse with a lightning bolt shaved into its forehead.
I remember the garbage bags full of soaked carpet and cushion
from my youth in the day and in the night,
when it feels like I have been carrying bodies around with me.
And I have. And I am.
The comeuppance we deliver is slant,

it takes years to come around
and then one day the string quartet manufactures the avalanche
and there we are, engulfing those standing around
a Camaro, striking matches off of stolen prosthetic limbs.
Take that, void-hearted faux.
Take that, horse-painted Camaro of time.
Take that, grey sky I carve into rock under.
Take that, comets and trolley cars
intent on altering my destiny.
What will become of us, my friend?
Sometimes we are phantasm vendors
roaming a wilderness where the trees look like people.
Sometimes we pass the skeleton of another Camaro
time has exhausted. I will quit smoking. I will quit dying,
but not today. Take that, daymares.
The sky is grey, but I am jubilant.
My head grows larger.
Sometimes I carry it beside me
like a suitcase. Sometimes I tie it with ribbon
that looks like duct tape
time chews at with its long fingernails,
as though it were filled with the very prosthetic limbs
lost teenagers pine for.
I'm glad you are here and we are not alone.
I just wanted you to know that.

I LOVE YOU, AND WE ARE ALL GOING TO DIE

It is the end of the world again
only this time it is the 5 AM variation
where sleep is rust

and you are the gleaming thing
that must wait for slow rain
and the air. The world is clearly ending,

just look at the light
starting to seep into the beyond.
We should arm ourselves with rope,

we should march into the sea,
we should miss forever the next person
we meet. We go to our next obligations

under the sign of exit music. The end
of the world? Nigh, as the night sky
dies into light O! it's a tank

just like the body although
the body is more a paper tank, so easily burned,
torn and written upon with the unspeakable

bent into words *tick* bursting into
flames *tick* at the instant of the assault *tick*
for which it was *tick* made. Had I the right

bone structure, I would fly
into your twilight this instant and lick your ear
right with honey. I would tell you something

you never remember precisely enough
to say, but as the scarred horizon starts to burn
toward you—for surely, *surely*

the world is ending—you keep building it
in your mouth as you remember
every single person you ever loved.

ALL SOULS PROCESSION

Bicycles dressed in animal suits
    thread double and triple-tiered parasols
spun in the ashen dusk,

    drums and rattles ask and ask.
Fabergé skulls wearing matadors and mistresses
    steal down 4th Avenue, brief anti-Lethe

upon a paved Lethe. One Lady Liberty
    is a shrouded effigy in a wheeled casket,
one a cloud-gowned girl

    trying to be still while perched
on a rusted car adorned with beads.
    At the mouth of the underpass,

urns hold flames which can't touch the darkness.
    Gold women dance prepositionally,
navigating yoked torches,

    and bandage-wrapped figures
with square feathers jutting from their masks
    lurch and glide on stilts and crutches

like forms moving over us in our dreams.
    A woman turns her head
and her head is the head of a giant wolf

    lacquered with mirror shards
so for a moment it is impossible to see yourself
    except broken and multiplied.

Somehow you are all still you. The train bleats
    like an exasperated gang of saxophones,
night's finished with us, we are confetti

    stepping into a burst of wind.
How we want. How we want
    to cup each haphazard flash

in the blurred photograph of our hands.

BAD MOVE, SIMON

You give an inch
and the sharks line up erosion facilitators
for miles, impatient to show off

their efficiency. You turn the other cheek
and look back to see your homeland
on fire, the smoke curling

into iconic representations
of the conquerors. There are worlds
where everything goes wrong.

Those worlds are here.
The clerk messes up your pickle order,
the transportation magistrate

mis-genders your photo ID.
You are asked to go someplace hot
and full of nails. You are forced.

Sand gets in the smoke
in your eyes. A thousand thousand
other decimations. You make-believe

toward a new world but a new world
is not enough, it perishes swiftly
like a match trying to ice skate.

The renegade spur of hope
is a peculiar spark
we contort like novice dancers to avoid.

With one touch it will catapult
the whole carnival into blazes,
the interlocutive environs stroked

with seedy appetite. Tonight
I hear the air pull itself through
the palm fronds. Tonight they are spears.

CHILD RECRUIT

Morning's a bramble invaded by crimson
blossoms and I am an airplane.
Peripheral vision's a muted bark
and I walk into trellis after thorny trellis
with pots and pans tangled in my landing gear.
I take Veteran's Day off to contemplate
my future and carve a tongue out of
my blood orange sorbet. The perfect time
to eat blood orange sorbet is not now
in the chilly now but compared to target
practice it is the perfect time to eat blood
orange sorbet with a freezing spoon
that sticks to my lip. My fatigues
fatigue my march toward the shooting range
and I feel my landing gear give beneath me
so I am on my belly in the dirt.
There is not enough air below my wings.
I am a very bad airplane and can only
play dangerous, unwinnable games
with the other anxiety machines.
One by one or all in clumps
I am asked to phantom my mates,
to clean the merry-go-round of others.
I have special goggles that let me see into
the heart of things. My wings grow sticky.
My blood orange sorbet refuses to melt
as it serpentines down my throat.
The sky won't come anywhere near me.

THIS RESURRECTION COSTS $4.95

Aren't you a photograph of a burning brook
turning slowly inside the glacier
of an old moment? Well,
now you are. In French exists the sentence
Les poètes se perdent dans les nuages
but this seems like a choice.
Don't you ice cream? A you
goes whistling like a missile through the world
or a music flown far ahead of us
as we try to explode out of the blocks.
Once, you say we are of the flood
but that this does not mean
that drought is not also prolific.
Can't this refrigerator go any faster?
I think we *find* ourselves in clouds,
whether that means we wake in bolts of mist
with some measure of surprise
or that we must concentrate in the midst
of hundreds of rippling congregations of vapor
until the idea that is us comes clear.
This sun's reach is not so great.
This moon's clearly painted, clearly set piece.
How can we tickle the chariot?
Before the horizon's an inferno breathing heavy,
let's sit down to brunch in the old style,
the one where we look at each other.
To tell this story
you need to press your palm
against the moment

when the mountain meets the valley,
but first you must trust the ear of your hand.
Where do you keep going all my life?
Didn't you know I loved you
until I thought sparks would stream
from the breaks in the earth as you moved
over it? but instead here we are, blinking at menus
in this lush mechanism,
trying to make something true up
while snowballs and campaigns fall apart
like people.

O PASSENGER MANIFEST

Even as the seams unstitch,
the horse must gleam, must gallop
like diamonds flung through a shaft of light.
You should never ever I forget.
You should always always I think as I wake
with a chest full of dust at a dance marathon.
Be urbane like a flower girl past her elocution lessons
but country like a hat slurring mama
or a fading blue tattoo.
Pleasant, as in *seat 3-B converted to flotation wafer*
going over a waterfall yet rendering passenger non-paralyzed
pleasant. The bus is a colored cloud of ill portent
hanging by an axle disagreeing with a girder,
a baby tooth before before before.
Breath drops from the ceiling.
Clearly, you must move me.
It will not be clear
whether you need a regatta or an armada.
You may promenade with an autographed spine,
you may limp beneath the weight of the right feather.
Sentences are hints. Every word is a door
swinging open on interminable abominations
and indubitable pleasures.
There is need, want, ears like abandoned snail shells
ruined to molten scarlet by one memory
but then a plain human heart
but then eyes like pools of stars and corkscrews.
Clearly you must move me, infant tornado,
little little radio. We are so otherwise alone here,

so otherwise without you. You need not wear a little uniform.
Unless. Not bore we now, not now please.
The seat mouth loses its laminated safety cartoon mind.
O go down lifted and swinging
like that boy from Memphis, that mind-reader.
As the headphones follow the emergency exit door,
see the little girl pat her father's hand.
They say our lush cavalry cannot attend the gross politic,
the boxed social, the consumption
I mean the dilemma-pierced spirit
but I think you have the right calculator.
Let the aviary rush to and from the hospice. Selah.
Just this once
and then over and over
do me the music of getting off the ground,
lead me to the lake of being the slingshot,
the lake on the summer day
when the lake is clear and cool and the cliff
40 feet up. I mean being the galvanized instrument.
Only seconds remain, team.
Little plastic rams leap from a pedestal
etched with the word CELEBRATOR,
you are apple pie and bulletproof.
Struck, always struck, even a glimpse is a blow
fallen like an object which when dropped
resembles the bird you can't check off in the bird book.
There's no propeller on a bird this big
but who am I to say you didn't just see a propeller
swim into the sky, fearful as if the villagers came quickly

with their spears and their torches and their certainty.
I want your encyclopedia
to fight them. A glimmer resolves in a pale wing
yawning terribly but for a second.
I am lonely here but for a second. Now
the diagram of a joke about this cursèd brevity
which revels now and again in such blisses
as gods would blush to take.
I feel the seatbelt rattle and fray, threads reach for light.
I feel alright,
the wind like a finger
like a polished carving knife beckoning
and I need you, can't you see me flying from here?
Look at my such-a-busted-harp mouth, taken begging
against the force of the sudden air—

ELECTRIC COMPANY

Good night, stranger.
The welts risen in the abused sky
call out lacerations and rue, call out
and ungentle the shutters of the house—It's alright.
The ash does not yet enter your mouth,
the capering tide of razors remains an imaginary
biting into a far concentric
and only later will the end of one world or another
roll its player piano braille
into the tips of your fingers.
You wake before a delicious perishable,
a boulder pulses in the scullery of your attention.
Stranger, good night.
Your tongue is my tongue backwards,
your sweet my salt.
We skate awkward across an eye
through flora of exploding eyes
while folk in fleet memory
ascend and descend ladders,
phosphorescent and silvered, mute
with their mouths open.
There is a ferocity moving toward us
for which we do not have the proper gloves,
the right greatcoat,
the final, big-enough word.
Good night. The sun will be there
but there will be no newspaper. The moon
will rise, but there will be no nightclub.
The lightning we believed ours
will decathect itself from us.

We will charge through what we thought was the night
and what we prayed was the next morning
into what waits,
what advances even by not moving.
A glance is a gaze is a waving-goodbye-to.
Many-guised stranger, I love you.
Your night comes swift to my dawn
like a desperate, wasteful kiss
that tells me we are still alive,
and won't be.

ACKNOWLEDGMENTS

Grateful acknowledgment is made to the editors of the publications in which some of these poems first appeared:

32poems: "& I Don't Sleep, I Don't Sleep, I Don't Sleep Till It's Light"

Boston Review: "Attack Attack"

The Concher: "Jalopy Bellicose"

DIAGRAM: "Jason Bredle," "At the Edge of a Deep, Dark Wood, Re-Purposed Dolphin Speaks"

Forklift, Ohio: "Child Recruit," "Bad Move, Simon"

The Journal: "Electric Company"

Thanks are also due teachers, friends and family, whose support and insight is incalculable, and without whom any work I do would be lesser to the point of meaninglessness, far too many to name here. I would like to thank some particulars, however: Lynne McMahon. Nicky Beer and Jason Koo. The McKees, Perrins, Cosgrays, and Gwynns. Special thanks to Jason Bredle, Dominic Arizona Bonuccelli, and Ander Monson.

NOTES

The epigraph is from the Panic Strikes a Chord song "Rappaport Vs. the Jet (That Bombed the Grocery Store)," from the album *I Can See Electricity at the Proper Distance*. Panic Strikes a Chord is Jeremy Brightbill.

"& I Don't Sleep..." takes its title from a line in the Wolf Parade song "Shine a Light."

"This Was During My Animal Rescue Phase" is for Sarah Bromer.

"You Think You Will Never Ask to be Set on Fire Again" is for Jamie Warren.

"Jason Bredle" and "Jalopy Bellicose" are for Jason Bredle.

MARC MCKEE earned his MFA from the University of Houston, and is currently pursuing a PhD at the University of Missouri in Columbia, where he lives with his wife, Camellia Cosgray. His poems appear in *Boston Review*, *Conduit*, *Crazyhorse*, *DIAGRAM*, *LIT*, *Pleiades*, *Salt Hill*, and several other places.

❋

NEW MICHIGAN PRESS, based in Tucson, Arizona, prints poetry and prose chapbooks, especially work that transcends traditional genre. Together with DIAGRAM, NMP sponsors a yearly chapbook competition. Marc is the 2008 winner.

DIAGRAM, a journal of text, art, and schematic, is published bimonthly at <http://thediagram.com>. Periodic print anthologies are available from the New Michigan Press.

❋

COLOPHON

Text is set in a digital version of Jenson, designed by Robert Slimbach in 1996, and based on the work of punchcutter, printer, and publisher Nicolas Jenson.

www.ingramcontent.com/pod-product-compliance
Lightning Source LLC
Chambersburg PA
CBHW031430040426
42444CB00006B/763